Angels
&
Inner Demons

By Nikki Avila

Published by Paradisiac Publishing
http://www.paradisiacpublishing.com

Follow the Author on Instagram: @nikki.avila

ISBN: 978-0692899083

Foreword:

First off, thank you. Without you this wouldn't matter. To survive I must write, but to live? Well my calling is you and reminding you that no matter how it may seem at times you are never truly alone. It took me far too long to learn that and I didn't necessarily learn it through people I knew (though it often times felt like I knew them). I learned it from the beautifully written words these people created from thin air. I learned it every time tears poured down my face because I finally felt understood.

I hope, now, to do the same for you. I hope my pain brushes against yours and together they settle just a little bit. Enough so that you might breathe easier after reading this collection of poems. This is the worst of me. The raw. The real. The devastating.

I'm sure many of you have gone through much worse than I, but maybe my words will touch you regardless. That is my hope anyhow.

Love Always,

Nikki Avila

Angels

In the end, she realized

not everything broken should be fixed

Although she lay broken
she was more beautiful
that way. For when light
fractured through her
shattered heart instead
of one rainbow, there were
many.

Only in shattered mirrors

did she find her reflection

to be true.

Its fractured pieces sung

to her soul.

And the missing parts?

They called to her heart.

When you've been
obliterated, crushed,
shattered into a million
tiny pieces, not all
those broken bits are
meant to be picked back
up. Some should stay in
the dirt, left to die with
the old you – the weak
you.

On those days where the sky cracked open and the heavens cried she did not scurry inside and hide indoors like all the others. No, she stood in the middle of the chaos that so perfectly mirrored her and let the torrent wash her of her many sins.

Lying in bed that night, for the first time in what seemed like an eternity, the demons didn't assault me. They lay quiet, sleeping in my head as my heart relished its victory.

Finally, it succeeded where the brain never could; creating belief in myself.

I never wore a mask

like the others did.

Perhaps that is why

they found me strange.

His laughter was light

Its glorious beams reaching –

reaching into every corner

dispelling the darkness,

ridding the world of sin.

And didn't I have more than

my fair share of them –

Sins.

I found release in

the oddest places.

It started with saying

goodbye to you.

The fact remained:

she needn't someone

who understood her,

only a rare individual

that didn't equate

different to broken

and damn sure didn't

think she needed fixing.

Only accepting.

I became something new,

smoke in the air when I

ceased to burn for you.

I told myself I couldn't do it again. Repeated it like a mantra. Prayed to God, begging him not to put me through this again. I had nothing left. Nothing. I could give no more without being left a husk. And yet when you came along I found myself filled once again with love and I had no desire to keep it for myself.

there were so many voices in

her head – none of them hers –

drowning out the little voice in

her heart saying, "go for it"

I wasn't ready for it. Couldn't fathom the kindness in your eyes and the tenderness in your touch – hated you for it. Because it made me want you, desperately, and my little body could take no more disappointment.

I'm so dreadfully tired of

loving with a fierceness

that exhausts and finding

no nourishment to replenish

what I've wasted

I didn't need you. Never would.
But God how I wanted you. I
craved you the way mermaids do
legs, the way beast wants a taste
of beauty. You were my floating
lights and my once upon a dream.
No matter how I had no need, my
want made me choose you. And
isn't that better?

Your inability to love me taught me more than a thousand kisses ever could. The way you meticulously destroyed my very being was a lesson I couldn't learn with gentle hands. It was your brutality that broke me, but it was also the same thing that built me into what I am. And for that I thank you.

Somehow between the both of us
we were able to construct a whole
heart from the crumbling remains
of our own

You didn't have to be

the Sun.

Just one of its rays.

Shedding light on the darkness

that called me home.

You burned me to the g

                                    r

                                         o

                    e   u

              s   n

          o   d

but still I r   -- gray

blotting out the sun

You are not just your demons, darling. Nor your angels. Hand your heart to someone who will dance with both.

in your arms

my soul quieted

the chaos fled

and peace settled

so this is love?

My ribs stood no chance against the beast that resided inside. Every beat cracked the makeshift bars. Every breath gave it room to move. That damned infernal organ would not be caged.

I wasn't a religious person. Not by any means. But then your body covered mine. Under your lips I never said God more. It became a mantra, whispered again and again. How fervently I prayed when your hands found my hips. And when we became one I knew heaven.

...I was your most devoted convert

You were never a monster.

At least you didn't look like

one.

No teeth. No claws.

But you terrified me all the

Same.

You didn't need hands to hurt me. Your words were weapon enough. They alone needled between my ribs, pried them open and attacked the heart. Sharper than any blade, they eviscerated me and left my insides to wither and die. They were masters of humiliation. Drawing themselves against the tender flesh behind my knees, leaving me helpless at your feet. Each and every one became wounds destined to weep forever...

Forever ends now.

Her greatest strength lay in

her ability to love herself

when no one else seemed to.

I was an addict. Plain and simple. The needle was my closest friend. Sliding beneath pock marked flesh and penetrating my veins. Initial contact sent shivers down my spine. This is what I wanted. Needed with every vestige of my being. Cold metal to cool my feverish disposition. And cool it did. My temperature plummeted when clarity took hold and the decision my withdrawal addled mind made became clear to me. I did it again. And I was too late. Hope surged through me. Becoming one with the blood I pumped it into.

I was never stronger than you. Didn't measure up in any noticeable way. You had the muscle, the brute strength to make me obey. If only because of fear. But damn if I wasn't resilient. No matter the bruises. No matter the words and humiliation. I survived. Strong people don't break and I did. Too many times to count. But I'm still here. Where are you?

Rainbows are nothing but fractured light. And isn't fractured synonymous with broken? That's all you are, sweetie, purity made breathtaking.

I tell myself I was built for this. That I had a choice and chose solitary confinement. But I know better. No human was made to be this lonely. I know it, Zeus knew it. That's why he condemned us to forever searching for our other half. So, we can once again become a being with four arms, four legs, two faces, and a single heart. Without the other, without the attachment some call weakness, we are not complete.

Monsters aren't all that scary. Not
the ones you can see anyway. When
the claws lay bare and the teeth are
all you can see what is there to fear?
It's the monsters in the closet and
under the bed that terrify me.
Lying in wait, ready to strike when
your guard's down.

Show me your face, baby, every
monstrous angle. I promise I won't
run.

There was nothing quiet
about our ending. It was
knees hitting concrete,
bruises blossoming. It
was an erratic beat of the
heart. A gasp for breath.
A stream of tears.

It was a start, and not
a silent one at that.

and if we were permitted

to meet again I don't

think you'd recognize me.

I've killed myself so many

times since you

And what if I told you I wasn't fixable? That as broken as I was, that's how I was staying. Like a petrified tree, I would grow no more leaves. I could be hacked away or left to exist as I was. Could you love me then? Would you even want to try?

It was a lightning strike igniting not one match, but a thousand. They destroyed themselves in the depths of her. It was thunder booming. Creating fissures in her overfilled heart. It was a hurricane making easy work of her eyes. It had to escape, by any means necessary.

And herein lay the problem: there was too much love in too little of a body. She wasn't built to contain it all. It wasn't hers to hoard away. She was meant to give it freely and unconditionally. Yet when no one wanted it, it had to go somewhere. However excruciating the departure was, it was necessary.

She simply couldn't survive with so much unrequited love ...

You feel that? How your airway closes. How oxygen itself ceases to exist. The slow destruction of your existence...or what it could've been.

What the future could've been. What it could've held. Does it hurt? Is it absolutely excruciating. This goodbye that didn't have to be anything but hello.

Self-sabotage. Not mutually assured destruction. Because somehow, she'll be okay. But you won't ever be the same. All because you couldn't close an old door and walk through the one she held open for you.

You don't get to shatter me and claim
the rainbows. The destruction? That
was all you. The resulting beauty?
That was me.

I was all flaws

made up entirely of

shattered pieces

and leftovers

For your own sanity

you have to come to

terms with what

you'll never know...

She was positive it would burn. To have so much sunshine living in her. But it was the most wonderful feeling she'd ever experienced. Each ray of light eradicated a shadow. Until, at last, there was nowhere for the monsters to hide. Even clouds had no place in somewhere so well lit. If he could give her this was there anything left to impossible?

I didn't want to be your whole
world. Hell, I didn't have time
to be. But the moon among your
stars? A girl could hope.

There's something beautiful about being alone. An epiphany occurs in those endless hours of self-reflection. It was never about lighting a candle in the dark. It was about embracing it.

Life's so much more than a journey to "happy". It's an acceptance of grief and rage. Hate and sorrow. Life is about accepting that all your poems might be labeled "sad" because, well, so is life.

I could breathe just fine alone. The world
didn't stop. Nothing broke that wasn't
already in pieces. I didn't need you to
survive. Hell, I didn't need you to live.
I'd be just fine by myself. But fine was
all I'd ever be. There would be the past
and an endless string of today's. No future.
Not the one I hoped for anyway. The one
with you in it.

She wasn't blue skies and sunshine.
Her possibilities didn't present
themselves to those looking for easy.
Storm chasers were the only ones
who stood a chance.

Only those who saw beauty in
destruction could also see the
possibilities: just as endless as
clear skies.

Would her rains wash away your
sins? Or would her winds rip you
to shreds?

How tragic. This whole time she
feared she wasn't enough.
Genuinely believed that she
couldn't fulfill all his desires.
When in reality she was too much
for him to handle.

I refuse to apologize for the way I love.

Absolutely is the only option for me.

All she wanted was someone who would wipe off the makeup. She wanted someone to see her for the corpse she was and not expect anything more. No painted on smiles allowed. She needed some-one who would love her for her beautiful frown.

All this time

I forgot to

look for the

good in me

We ceased to be just bodies

when you looked into my eyes.

It became less about **excitement**

and more about **enlightenment**

She was simultaneously the darkness
of the tunnel and the light at the end.

Only she could free herself from this
nightmare.

Her silence screamed louder
than she ever could. A protest
of sorts. They would not change,
no matter the ruckus they made.

Original had no need for noise.

I don't know much about forever.

But a couple thousand right nows

with you ought to get us close

Inner Demons

I feel like I'll never be 100%.

Too much of me is scar tissue now.

I was too much for you
so you tore me apart at the
seams, discarding the pieces
you feared touching. Those
that were exquisite in their
rawness, those that could've
brought you to your knees.

in the bowels of me

a cage sits

holding a beast

that begs release

so it can

love you

once more

When I was made of straw

their words caved my resolve to live

and so, I rebuilt myself out of sticks.

But his cruelty was more than I could take

and my fortress collapsed in on itself.

Yet again I rebuilt myself anew

this time from nearly impenetrable brick.

No one has touched me since.

she couldn't stand to be touched

to have someone's hands cup her cheek

or graze her arms. fear struck her every time,

prepared her for the viselike grip and bruises.

someone who once loved nothing more

than to cuddle shied away from the barest

brush of skin on skin

And wasn't she tired?

Of nothing in particular.

Just being alive.

The what-ifs kept her awake

at night. Sending her mind

down the roads not taken. Making

her analyze every decision that

brought her here, to the present.

They haunted her. Destroyed her

sense of reality. And left her

but a husk of herself. Those

what-ifs stole her today's

and tomorrow's and dragged

her back to the past.

in all pain

poetry can

be found

Like a flower, once plucked

she quickly withered away

Color faded from her once

extraordinary petals. And

her stem wilted, collapsing

under the strain of confinement.

If they'd only known how their

words would change her.

If they could see the scars

that marked her.

Perhaps they wouldn't have

been so cruel.

She purged her demons

with ink stained hands

and paper cuts.

I ripped out my fucking heart

for you. Served it to you on

a silver platter. Destroyed who

I was for you and recreated

myself into someone you could

love. And dammit if it still

wasn't enough.

How I worshipped you. Kicking myself
when you knocked me down and telling
you it was okay. Kissing your cracked
and bleeding knuckles with bruises
marring my face. Kneeling before you
as you ripped out my intestines. Only
to leave them rotting on the dirty
floor. How foolishly I loved you.

Just once she wanted

to be enough

To have someone crave all

she desperately wished

to give

But the world just wasn't ready

for her kind of love –

Selfless

Sometimes all you have is the

fire that burns inside.

And if the kindling's anger?

So be it.

The monsters he left me with?

They growl, howl, scream for

release. Pull at their chains –

the ones I created for sanity's

sake. Whisper vile thoughts

to me – about me.

Inner demons. He created them.

Fed them. Grew them.

Then left them – to torture me.

But he didn't walk away empty

handed. He took something with

him. Something vital. My ability

to love … me.

Oh how I would like to

remember myself

But time changed that

little girl

And pain forged her into a

woman

And when you left

I broke down –

tears streaming down

my face, hands

clutching my chest

because I could

finally breathe.

Doubt was her constant companion,

a gift from those who

brought her very

existence into

question.

Life has a funny way of

making death look desirable...

The past shattered her.

Destroying everything

she knew to be true.

But it was only during

that destruction that

she learned what it was

to be strong in the

face of adversity,

to hold compassion

close when hate seeks to

thrive, and most importantly

her own worth. And so

she held no hate for the

past, only gratitude.

And life broke her

repeatedly

until at last she learned

to stand.

How is it that I survive
when there's so little left
of me still alive?

There are no parts

of me left unscarred,

untouched, unbroken

But if real is your

desire, I'm the one

for you.

There are days paper

alone sends me into

a fright and pens

become monsters.

It's those days I

need them the most.

The days when

I terrify myself.

only the ocean knows the eternity

of my pain

what it is to exist without ever

being understood

to have people look upon you with

fear and awe

but never truly be willing to dive below

the surface

I wasn't a puzzle.

That would imply

all the pieces fit.

Or that they were

all present.

You were endless possibilities,

a future I couldn't imagine.

But you could and you

decided to give me hell.

You were a cigarette

calling my name at all times

stealing the breath from my lungs

poisoning me from the inside out

leeching every ounce of good from my life

but I was addicted to the very thought of you

no matter how your touch killed

I wasn't one to give up. Didn't walk away from broken things. But being with you was giving up on me. It was more than spider web veins through my soul. It was forfeiting whole pieces of it.

I cried more for me when I
laid in your arms than I did for
you when I slept alone

you desired me for all you saw on

the outside – sunshine & rainbows

but once my insides spilled before

you – predators that lurk under beds

and in closets, your undying love for

me quickly vanished & another

monster took the place I reserved

for you

How much more sand

must f

    a

      l

       l

before your name isn't

followed by physical

pain?

I didn't know Heaven could

be Hell until memories of

you scorched my heart.

Her soul

gave hell

a run for

its money

Slice my tender flesh to ribbons

of red. Paint me black and blue.

But please leave my heart

unscathed.

my soul was a battle ground. one

where the head attacked the heart.

where the heart disregarded thought.

both out for blood. both dooming me.

every night I pray for rest.

not for my aching body but

for my tortured soul.

This me I've become isn't
really me at all and I think
that's the saddest part.

If screaming alone would stop their poking and prodding, their incessant need to pull her apart and build her anew, she might never stop. If a raw throat and a useless voice would win her the freedom she needed like air then she'd give it freely. Anything to be rid of these shackles.

life was her riptide

forever dragging her back

to the hell she already

escaped

Your love wasn't freeing or beautiful. It was manacles tearing my skin with the slightest movement away from you. It was the ugly scars the spikes left. Raised and infected. You were no lover but a jailor. Caging me to keep me close when all I wanted was the air outside my cell.

I craved insanity. Would rather a broken mind than having to suffer through another memory of you.

you're worse than the devil

not content with my soul

but desiring my body and

heart too.

how is it that you're

dead and gone

but I'm the carcass?

why am I the one

rotting away when

worms slither through you?

when will my

hell end and

yours begin?

or was death your

way out? An

escape from what

you left me with? Weeping

wounds and a

shattered soul

These scars don't mean healed. They
mean changed. The puckered tissue
isn't a testament to wars won, but
battles lost. Each one a piece of me
I had to let go to survive you.

Contain your vile words, monster.

There's nothing you can say I

haven't said to myself a 1000 times

over.

Emotions built my grave. 6 feet of hate. Burrowed down deep. The first shovel full of dirt is laced with depression. And the next. And the next. Once more. So much depression. Followed by grief no one believes I'm capable of. Pain that transcends my age. Self-loathing and humiliation. Doubt because of YOU and YOU and YOU.

Emotions built my grave but people pushed me in. With their thoughtless words of "advice". Making sure I understand what I can and can't feel. What I can and can't know. How they invalidate this agony. How they call me naïve and brush aside the shroud of depression. If only it were that easy!

But I feel! I feel and feel until hope can't exist in this whirlwind of emotions. So fragile. So breakable. It withers beneath the pressure. It's only me. This grave. And the cold dirt seeping into my mouth.

I killed you.

The memories of your smile

however rare that was

your lingering touch

that place in my heart

I crushed you with forget

purged you from my soul

the name, the date, the time

all gone

all but this, this

monster that looks

so much like you

except that smile

What too many fail to realize

is people aren't just broken...

someone has to break them

Smoke, to me, represented strength.

It was the part of destruction that

lived on...I don't believe that anymore.

I know better.

Smoke is nothing but a shade, a poor

substitution of the fire that once blinded

that once consumed

that once mesmerized.

Smoke is the me I am now.

Less than I was before.

Burned up and dissipating... g o n e

You dug my grave

but I climbed in.

Death was preferable

to you.

It took me a long time to stop blaming you. And some days I still do. Some nights too. When the lights go out and the shadows recede I can't help but curse your name. If I blame you for the pain then I can put the cold sheets on you too. And the empty house. Maybe even the lonely dinners. If I give all that to you, perhaps I can finally sleep.

The most excruciating part? For a moment, just a moment, the chaos settled. In your arms there was safety from the demons. No matter how they tried, they couldn't touch me.

Now you're one of them. Your smile torments. The memory of the peace you wrought fuels them. You were calm and storm. Different in all the ways I hadn't planned for.

When the pains too heavy

and the torments too much

I crawl in bed and hide.

How useless it is though:

crawling under covers

you can't hide from what's inside.

There's just this feeling. Its wholly indescribable but completely present. It's that irritation in your throat, that nausea in your stomach that tells you something isn't right. It's the sickness before it incapacitates you. The cold. The flu. Except it's not. Because you aren't sick. There's no medicine to fix what you have. There's no diagnoses other than different. You don't belong.

I didn't realize, didn't suspect, didn't
know it was you. My mind was else-
where. With the school and the work
and the demands. It couldn't have been
you. Responsibilities. That's what it
was. My life was a balancing act. It
wasn't you. Yet when you fell, when
I could hold on no longer, it was then
that I began to breathe.

I read this quote about grief being nothing more than unspent love trying to find an escape. So what of those moments when I grieve for myself? For the little girl left behind and the naïve child that's no more. Did I forget to love them? Is the love I hold for them now useless? Like the hugs you ache to give to the dead.

Let me boil it down for you:

being **protective** is keeping

harm from that which you love.

being **possessive** is being harmful

to that which you love.

It's really quite simple.

Who knew radio silence

could be so destructive?

I'd rather you yelled,

cursed, called me names

at least then you'd be

talking to me

Was it too much to ask,

too much to expect that

I'd be allowed to be my

own artist?

I don't think "almost" is the
saddest word in the dictionary.
I think "almost" is the worst
feeling known to man.

I was almost enough…

Alone never bothered me. It was my break from the world. My safe haven from me. It was when I was around people that it struck. This hunger like no other. Eating everything I had to give and more. I didn't want to be anymore. To simply exist...no. I didn't want to be a person among people or another voice disturbing the air. I wanted to be more than a body, more than sound. I needed to matter. To fit. To belong.

Alone never bothered me. It was rooms full of people that killed all I had to give and more. It was a smile painted on a corpse and passed off as real. Because they never noticed or didn't care to mention how death hung around me like a friend. I didn't want to be another person among people...well I wasn't. I was a cancer, devouring myself from the inside out. I was lonely.

Pain didn't scare me anymore. Hurt was the least of my worries. What I was afraid of now was that I might never heal. There's only so many beatings a person can take before they're permanently altered.

Sure, people treat you how you treat yourself.

But sometimes you treat yourself how people

treat you.

Some days I feel so little and I
wonder how I'm alive.
Other days the beating of my heart is
painful enough to make me wish I wasn't.

Most nights I sleep on my stomach. Those nights I'm carefree and exhausted. Other nights I sleep with my books and desk in view, cuddled up and content. Then there are nights I do neither. I just curl into myself and face the wall. Hide under the blankets and pretend the worlds not real. Because if it's not real then neither is my pain.

The thing is there's different kinds of done. There's feel good done. I can finally breathe done. Want to be done. Then there's have to be done. The done you choose because you deserve better. It's the painful kind that keeps you awake at night.

It wasn't so much an opposition to speaking.
Not an aversion either. Quite the opposite.
Words clawed at her throat, attempting to find
escape. But one too many times she painted
on that pathetic smile. One too many times
she pretended. She pretended so well that the
only words she could now speak were "I'm
okay"

I don't know if it's the lingering

pain that's got me so d

                    o

                w

                    n

or if sad is just my disposition

The time has come for me to stop blaming you. Sure, you planted the seeds but I watered them and brought them into the light. Cherished as gifts, I gave them a home in my heart. Even after you left, I let them stay. Free of charge. Because they were all I had left of you. Memories of your smile faded. Your laugh ceased its echo long ego. The warmth you brought quickly turned cold. But the demons? They were more resilient. Because I let them be.

Was there ever a moment, however infinitesimal, that you considered releasing me? A moment in which you realized that no matter the love you claimed to feel, it didn't show. Did you ever think to help me let go? Because we were both well aware I couldn't, wouldn't, do it on my own. Or was this end pre-determined? A total destruction of you and me.

She sought to be a flower

of the f

      a

        l

         l

those that gave their

pretty petals

to the dirt

whose stems failed to

support & crumpled in

on themselves

A flower of the

decaying kind.

Dying so that

others might live.

Yes, she thought

that wonderfully fitting.

I needn't a rope

your words were

noose enough

it's ironic how

full empty can

make you feel.

surely, I'd be

hollow without

its presence

Happiness was my

chemo

And what an epic failure

it was.

A Note from the Author:

Congratulations! You muddled through my mind and survived. By now you've learned a couple things about me. First and foremost: I've got a hell of a lot more demons than angels. Second: I'm still here. And so are you.

What you wouldn't have learned is why. Why is it that I put pen to paper and turn pain into poetry? I was fourteen, bullied and needing an outlet. Diaries were a thing beyond my capabilities. I couldn't write about myself. Not really. Poems were doable. They were vague, unclaimed and therapeutic.

As the years went by and the bullying stopped so did I. I stopped writing the morbid, melancholic and dark. Then it happened: life. It flipped me upside down, turned me inside out, and threw everything I couldn't handle at my face. I needed to cope. I needed a way to express all the torment change wrought. But more than that, I needed people to know without really telling them.

I still haven't. Perhaps I never will. Something shifted during the darkest period in my life (so far) and I found words joined me in the present. They begged for the release I refused to give.

You don't have to either. I suppose that's what I'm trying to get at. Keep your secrets, if you'd like. Keep the anger and the pain and the grief. But don't, please don't, bottle them up inside. They'll kill you.

Write. Write poetry. Write short stories. Write a novel. Write letters you'll never give away. Just let the human language spread a balm across your wounds. And when you're ready, if you ever are, share the magic you've made.

Sincerely,

A Fellow Outcast